PICCOLO BOOK OF RIDDLES

D1428716

PICCOLO BOOK OF RIDDLES

S. B. CUNNINGHAM

Text illustrations by Karen Heywood
Cover illustration by Martin Knowelden

A Piccolo Original
Pan Books London and Sydney

First published 1973 by Pan Books Ltd,
Cavaye Place, London SW10 9PG
5th printing 1975
ISBN 0 330 23642 3
© S. B. Cunningham 1973

Printed in Great Britain by
Richard Clay (The Chaucer Press) Ltd, Bungay, Suffolk

I would like to thank all my friends whom I badgered for months to give me riddles, and who made this book possible.

Especially, Mrs Wiggins and the third-formers of Midhurst Intermediate School, who not only collected riddles but made up some good ones of their own; Andrew Cunningham, Matthew Letts, the Barker family and Dave Brier who bothered to write them down for me; and the children of Midhurst Grammar School and the Herbert Shiner School in Petworth.

The source of many of the older and rhyming riddles is Professor A. Taylor's marvellous book, *English Riddles from Oral Tradition*, for which I am very grateful.

The author and publishers would like to thank the University of California Press for permission to use the following riddles from Professor A. Taylor's ENGLISH RIDDLES FROM ORAL TRADITION: *Six legs, two heads, two hands and a nose* p 11, *Crooked as a rainbow* p 14, *I move without wings, In yonder valley, I tremble at each breath of air* p 17, *Brass button, Long and slinky like a trout* p 19, *Long slim and slender* p 20, *A little house full of meat* p 45, *Patch upon patch* p 47, *Two black-white doves* p 48, *Runs over fields and woods all day* p 50, *As I went over Heepo Steeple* p 71, *The Queen of Morocco* p 80, *Mr Huddle* p 92, *Old Father Boris* p 94, *Its belly is a boat* p 97, *A certain maiden* p 98, *What is it that falls down a cliff, A house full of grey wool, I threw it from a minaret,* p 99, *What must have* p 112.

WHAT ARE RIDDLES?

When first I appear I seem mysterious,
But when I'm explained, I'm nothing serious.

That's a riddle about a riddle!

You wouldn't think, perhaps, that guessing the right
answer to a riddle could be a matter of life and death?
Well, it used to be. There were some very strange ones
called 'neck-riddles', for the good reason that your very
neck could depend on them. They were made up by crimi-
nals, and if their judges couldn't guess the answer, then
they were set free. So as you can imagine they tended to be
very difficult riddles indeed. (Try that out, the next time
you're in trouble!)

And then there was the Sphinx. I expect you know her –
the terrible monster with a woman's head and the body of
a lion. She terrorized the countryside around Thebes in
Greece, thousands of years ago, and all because of this
riddle: What goes on four legs in the morning, two legs at
noon, and three legs in the evening?

It was fairly important to know the answer to that one,
because if you didn't you were eaten alive by the Sphinx.

She ate up lots of bad riddlers, until at last Oedipus
found the answer. It is a man: he goes on all fours as a
baby, two legs as an adult, and walks with a stick as an
old man.

Every country has its own tradition of riddles. They have
been passed down through the generations by word of
mouth – and not just by children, either. Riddles were a
very grown-up business and everybody told them. The
Mongolians, the Russians, the Greeks, the Polynesians,
they've all got their own riddles, and the odd thing is, not

that so many of them are different, but that so many of them are nearly the same.

Take Humpty Dumpty.

He's an egg, and he's been rolling all over Europe for hundreds of years under different names. In Saxony they called him Humpelken Pumpelken. In Ireland they called him Roili, Roili. But wherever he was, no one could put him together again.

Here's an old one you can find all over the world.

Q. The man who made it did not want it; the man who bought it did not use it; the man who used it did not know it. What is it?

If you don't know the answer to that one, I'll keep the secret, just to annoy you, but I will give you a clue. The man at the end doesn't know it, because he is dead!

Did you guess it? If you did, it's quite a powerful feeling of discovery, isn't it? And if you didn't, then I expect you feel as I do when I can't work something out – an irritation, a wanting to know, for someone to give the answer. Which is why riddles have power. And why they are used in secret rites, and initiation ceremonies, and religions. (What about the strange Christian riddle of: Three in one, and one in three?)

And of course, riddles come in very useful if you want to conceal something – like secret writing in a diary, for instance, and codes and ciphers, and passwords. The early Christians used the sign of a fish, because their word for fish was made up of the initial letters of Christ's titles. It was a kind of 'in' sign, for people in the know. (And come to think of it, what about inn-signs – lots of them have turned into riddles – do you know what Goat and Compasses really means? God encompasses.) That's why I have put rhyming slang into a riddle book.

I love the old ones, so I've put some of them in this book too. A lot of them are in rhyme, because that's how people remembered them best. A lot of them are just pictures in words – just as we might say, 'That's a mackerel-sky,' when the wind has broken up the clouds into little pieces. Call the sky 'a mackerel' and that's a riddle. (Or a metaphor.)

The Latvians talk about the sky at night as a 'blue blanket, full of ears of wheat.' The Indians call it 'a woman coming in the evening, dressed in innumerable pearls.' Both riddling ways of describing the dark and the stars. (Shakespeare saw that the sky was the floor of heaven, 'thick inlaid with patines of bright gold'.)

But maybe you like the funny ones best?

Riddles seem to have taken a very funny turn lately. For all I know the Anglo-Saxons thought their riddles were a scream – but they are nothing compared to nowadays ones. More like jokes than riddles, but more fun. (And impossible to find the answer – at least I can't.)

Still, don't forget that in 1511 this riddle was published:

Q. How many calves' tails behoveth to reach from the earth to the sky?

A. No more but one, an it be long enough.

And if that isn't the same as the one about – How many balls of string does it take to reach the moon? One, if it's long enough – then I'm an astronaut.

Anyway, here are some riddles – and you can make your own book of the ones I've left out.

By the way, the answer to that other one is – a coffin!

HAVE YOU HEARD THIS ONE?

Q. What asks no questions, but receives lots of answers?
A. A telephone.

Q. What question can never be answered Yes?
A. Are you asleep?

Q. If I should catch a newt, why is it bound to be smaller than yours?
A. Because it would be my newt (minute).

Q. Who was the fastest runner in the world?
A. Adam. He was the first in the human race.

> What's big and loud,
> But never talks.
> He chews up corn,
> And spits out the stalks?
> A. ˙ɹǝʇsǝʌɹɐɥ-ǝuᴉqɯoɔ A

Q. How did little Bo-peep lose her sheep?
A. She had a crook with her.

Q. A woman who works in a sweetshop in Birmingham has measurements of 42 – 26 – 48. She is 5 feet 4 inches tall, and wears size ten shoes. What do you think she weighs?
A. She weighs sweets.

Q. What plays when it works, and works when it plays?
A. A fountain.

Q. Did you ever hear the story of the red-hot poker?
A. You couldn't grasp it.

> Pray tell me, ladies, if you can,
> Who is this highly favoured man,
> Who though he has married many a wife,
> May still be single all his life?
> A. A clergyman.

Q. Did you ever hear the story of the new roof?
A. It's way over your head.

Q. What's the surest way of doubling a pound?
A. Fold it.

Q. Why does a donkey eat thistles?
A. Because he's an ass.

Q. What do bees do with all their honey?
A. They cell it.

> Six legs, two heads, two hands and a nose,
> But uses only four legs as it goes.
> A. Man on horseback.

Q. Why does a duck go into the water?
A. For divers reasons.

Q. Why does he come out again?
A. For sun-dry reasons.

Q. Why did the butcher put a lot of bread in his sausages?
A. Because he couldn't make both ends meat.

Q. What did the policeman say when he trod on a banana?
A. The next of skin have been informed.

MEET THE BIGGER FAMILY

Q. A man whose name was Bigger, got married. Who was bigger, Mr Bigger or Mrs Bigger?

A. Mr Bigger, because he had always been Bigger.

Q. They had a little boy, and they called him John. Now who was the bigger, Mr Bigger, Mrs Bigger or John?

A. John Bigger, because he was a little bigger.

Q. All three of them went to a wedding on Saturday, and had their picture taken. Mr Bigger was standing next to Mrs Bigger, and son John was next to his mother. Which was the biggest then?

A. Mrs Bigger, because she was by father bigger.

Q. When Mr Bigger died, Mrs Bigger married another Mr Bigger. Who was the bigger then, Mrs Bigger or the new Mr Bigger?

A. Mrs Bigger, because she was twice bigger.

Q. When the second Mr Bigger died, they buried him by the old mill stream. Who was the biggest then?

A. Mr Bigger, by a damn site.

Q. But as the years went by, Mrs Bigger's love for Mr Bigger never died. Who was the bigger then?

A. Neither. As Mrs Bigger said: 'This thing is bigger than both of us.'

I SAY! I SAY! I SAY!

Q. What did the North wall say to the West wall?
A. Meet you at the corner.

Q. Why was Cinderella thrown out of the hockey team?
A. Because she ran away from the ball.

Q. What did the bus-conductor say to the one-legged man?
A. Hop on, sir.

Q. What did the big chimney say to the little chimney?
A. You're too young to smoke.

> Crooked as a rainbow, slick as a plate,
> Ten thousand horses can't pull it straight.
> A. ˙ɹǝʌᴉɹ ∀

Q. What did the leaning tower of Pisa say to Big Ben?
A. If you've got the time, I've got the inclination.

Q. What did the piece of wood say to the electric drill?
A. You bore me.

Q. Why is a rock braver than a mountain?
A. Because it is a little boulder.

Q. What did the hat say to the scarf?
A. You hang around, and I'll go on ahead.

Q. What did the pig say when the man got him by the tail?
A. This is the end of me.

Q. Why is the nose in the middle of the face?
A. Because it's the scenter.

Q. Why can't you remember the last tooth you had taken out?
A. It went right out of your head.

Q. What did the big toe say to the little toe?
A. There's a heel following us.

Q. Why does a coat get larger when it is taken out of a suitcase?
A. Because when you take it out you find it in creases.

Q. What has a hundred legs but cannot walk?
A. Fifty pairs of trousers.

Q. What has four legs and flies?
A. A dead horse – and two pairs of trousers.

Q. Three large women went walking under one umbrella, but none of them got wet. Why?
A. It wasn't raining.

Q. What would happen to a man if he swallowed his teaspoon?
A. He wouldn't be able to stir.

Q. What did the trumpet say?
A. Well, I'll be blowed!

Q. What did the ram say to his girl-friend?
A. I love ewe.

Q. What did the big telephone say to the little telephone?
A. You're too young to be engaged.

Q. Why does Father Christmas go down the chimney?
A. Because it soots him.

Q. What did his followers say when Moses had a row with his brother?
A. Keep yer Aaron, Moses.

Q. What kinds of fish do you wear on your shoes?
A. Soles and eels.

Q. What is a metronome?
A. A little man in the Paris underground.

Q. What's the difference between an elephant and a flea?
A. Elephants can have fleas, but a flea can't have an elephant.

Q. What usually runs in the family?
A. Noses.

Q. Why were the two red blood cells so unhappy?
A. They loved in vein.

Q. What's the fish frier's best friend?
A. The chip monk.

Q. How do you make a Venetian blind?
A. Poke his eyes out.

Q. When did the Chinaman go to the dentist?
A. Tooth-hurtee.

Q. Why does lightning shock people?
A. Because it doesn't know how to conduct itself.

WHAT CAN IT BE?

Lives in winter,
Dies in summer,
And grows with its root upward!
A. Icicle.

I move without wings
Between silken strings,
I leave as you find,
My substance behind.
A. Spider.

Q. What kind of coat is made without buttons and put on
   wet?
A. A coat of paint.

In yonder valley there runs a deer,
With golden horns and silver hair.
It's neither fish, flesh, feather nor bone;
In yonder valley it runs alone.
A. Sun.

I tremble at each breath of air,
And yet can heaviest burdens bear.
A. Water.

Q. What strikes but never hits?
A. Lightning.

Q. What stands still on a hill?
A. A house.

Q. Dai (pronounced Di), the milkman was called Dai the Milk. But then he started putting water into it. What did they call him then?

A. Dai Lute.

Q. What was Emlyn the Communist called?

A. Emlyn Kremlin.

Q. And Baxter the bricklayer?

A. Baxter the Wall.

Q. Berry was a woodsman. What did they call him?

A. Berry the Hatchet.

Q. Boult was a locksmith, so they called him . . .?

A. Boult the Door.

Q. And what did they call Carrie, the porter?

A. Carrie the Bag.

ASK ME ANOTHER

Brass button,
Blue coat,
Can't catch a billy-goat.
A. Policeman.

Long and slinky like a trout,
Never sings till its guts come out.
A. Gun.

What God never sees,
What the Queen seldom sees,
What we see every day,
Read this riddle, I pray.
A. An equal.

If you feed it, it will live;
If you give it water, it will die.
A. Fire.

The sharp slim blade,
That cuts the wind.
A. Grass.

Q. Who earns his living without doing a day's work?
A. A nightwatchman.

Q. When is it a good thing to lose your temper?
A. When it's a bad one.

Q. What can't you hold for ten minutes, though it is lighter than a feather?
A. Your breath.

Q. How can you get into a locked cemetery at night?
A. With a skeleton key.

Q. What is bought by the yard, but worn out by the foot?
A. A carpet.

Q. Which has more legs, a cow or no cow?
A. No cow. A cow has four legs, but no cow has eight legs.

Q. When is a goat nearly?
A. When it is all butt.

Q. How many peas in a pint?
A. 1 P.

Q. What makes the tower of Pisa lean?
A. It never eats.

Q. If a bird is run over by a lawn mower, what do you get?
A. Shredded tweet.

Q. If crocodile skins make good shoes, what do banana skins make?
A. Good slippers.

Q. Why did the Romans build straight roads?
A. Because they didn't want to drive their horses round the bend.

> Long slim and slender,
> Dark as homemade thunder,
> Keen eyes and peaked nose,
> Scares the Devil wherever it goes.
> A. Snake.

Q. What did the Children of Israel have to eat in the desert?
A. The sand which is there (sandwiches).

Q. And where did they get them?
A. Ham was sent there with his followers, who were bred and mustered, and when Lot's wife was turned into a pillar of salt, all but her (butter) went into the desert.

Q. Why are blacksmiths undesirable citizens?
A. Because they forge and steel.

Q. How many weeks belong to the year?
A. Forty-six; the other six are only Lent.

Q. What ship is always fastened to a pier?
A. Lordship.

Q. What runs round a field but does not move?
A. A hedge.

Q. Why is a lawyer like a ballet dancer?
A. They both practise at the bar.

Q. Why do the Yeomen of the Guard never eat fish on Fridays?
A. They're Beefeaters.

Q. A farmer had no chickens; nobody ever gave him any; he never bought, borrowed, begged or stole any; yet he had 2 eggs for breakfast every morning. How?
A. He had ducks.

Q. Why is an inheritance like a bee looking for honey?
A. They are both bequests.

Q. What has many keys that fit no locks?
A. A piano.

Q. Many men am I, but only one long arm.
A. The law.

Q. If a man is born in Turkey, grows up in Italy, goes to America, and dies in London, what is he?
A. Dead.

Q. Which moves faster, heat or cold?
A. Heat. You can catch cold.

Q. Why is snow different from Sunday?
A. It can fall on any day of the week.

Q. What hasn't got a mouth, yet smokes a pipe?
A. A stove.

WHAT'S ALL THIS THEN?

Q. Do you know the riddle about the bed?
A. It hasn't been made yet.

Q. Why did the chicken cross the road?
A. For its own fowl reasons.

Q. What did Jack Frost say to the violet?
A. Wilt thou? And it wilted.

Q. How far can you go into the woods?
A. To the middle; after that you will be going out.

We have a horse
Without any head,
And all dressed up,
Not living or dead.
A. Clothes-horse.

Q. If I were to see you standing beside a donkey, what fruit would I think of?
A. A pear (pair).

Q. Why does a clock never strike thirteen?
A. He hasn't the face to do so.

Q. Where does Friday come before Thursday?
A. In the dictionary.

Q. What happens to a boy when he misses the last bus home?
A. He catches it when he gets back!

What is it,
A rich man has and wants more of,
A fat man has and doesn't want,
And a poor man wants and can't get?
A. Pounds.

Q. What does the QE2 weigh just before leaving Southampton?
A. Anchor.

Q. Why should you always remain calm when you meet cannibals?
A. Well, you don't want to get into a stew, do you?

Q. If a boy ate his father and mother, what would that make him?
A. An orphan.

ANIMAL CRACKERS

Q. What lives in the woods and is highly dangerous?
A. A crow with a machine gun.
Q. What is small and hairy and has six legs?
A. An ant with a fur coat on.
Q. What is small as a pinprick and jumps like a kangaroo?
A. A flea with baseball boots on.
Q. What sits on a lily-pad and says, 'Cloak, cloak?'
A. A chinese flog.
Q. What goes 999 plonk?
A. A millipede with a wooden leg, waiting for an ambulance.
Q. If you put three ducks in a crate, what do you have?
A. A box of quackers.

QUIPS AND QUIRKS

Q. What is it you need most in the long run?
A. Your breath.

Q. What does a fish do when it's desperate?
A. Throws itself out of the river.

Q. What are you doing when you sleep soundly?
A. Snoring.

Q. A man was in the middle of the Pacific, and yet only 3 miles from the nearest land. How was that?
A. It was three miles *down*.

Q. Why did the secretary file the letters?
A. She'd lost her scissors.

Q. Why does a glowworm glow?
A. He only eats light meals.

Q. How do you get 4 elephants in a mini?
A. 2 in the front, and 2 in the back!

Q. Why do elephants wear hats?
A. So they can't be seen in a crowd.

Q. What did the grizzly take on holiday with him?
A. All the bear essentials.

Q. Why did the moonbeam?
A. Because it saw the skylark.

Q. What goes up a chimney down, but won't come down a chimney up?
A. An umbrella.

Q. Why do carpenters believe there's no such thing as stone?
A. They never saw it.

Q. Why is a baby worth its weight in gold?
A. Because it's a dear little thing.

YOU MUST BE JOKING!

What's the best way of proving a point? Stick it into your finger, of course! But it doesn't have to be that painful. Have a go at these . . .

Q. Can you prove that a cat has three tails?
A. No cat has two tails. One cat has one more tail than no cat. Therefore one cat has three tails. Simple!

Q. Can you prove that Nelson was a coward?
A. Yes. The last thing Nelson did was to die for his country, and that's about the last thing a coward will do.

Q. Can you prove that a loaf of bread is the mother of an engine?
A. Easy. Bread is a necessity. An engine is an invention. And necessity is the mother of invention. Therefore bread is the mother of an engine.

Q. How can you prove that twice ten is the same as twice eleven?
A. Because twice ten is twenty, and twice eleven is twenty too (two).

Q. Can you prove that a dumb man can speak, and a blind man see?

A. Yes. Because the dumb man picked up a bicycle wheel and spoke, and a blind man picked up a hammer and saw.

Q. Can you prove that it's dangerous to go into the woods in springtime?

A. Because the grass has blades, the flowers have pistils, the leaves shoot, the cowslips about, and the bulrush is out.

Q. Can you prove that the wind is the sea?

A. The wind is invisible; in visible is a b; bees are insects; in sects is C; therefore the wind is the sea.

Q. Can you prove that a carriage is nothing?

A. Yes. A carriage is a trap; a trap is a gin; gin is a spirit; a spirit is a ghost; and a ghost is nothing.

I saw a peacock with a fiery tail
I saw a blazing comet drop down hail
I saw a cloud wrapped with ivy round
I saw an oak creep upon the ground
I saw an ant swallow up a whale
I saw the sea brimful of ale
I saw a Venice glass full fifteen feet deep
I saw a well full of men's tears that weep
I saw red eyes all of a flaming fire
I saw a house bigger than the moon and higher
I saw the sun at twelve o'clock at night
I saw the man that saw this wondrous sight.

Can this be true?

Q. How can you tell the naked truth?
A. Just give the bare facts.

Q. How can you always find a liar out?
A. By going to his house when he isn't in.

Q. How can you put a horse on his mettle?
A. Shoe him.

Q. Why should you never describe an animal as a cart-horse?
A. Because you shouldn't put the cart before the horse.

Q. Why should you never tell a secret in a vegetable garden?
A. Because the potatoes have eyes, the corn has ears, and the beanstalk.

Q. What was the wife of the engineer called?
A. Bridget.

Q. How can you do comparatively well in life?
A. Get on, get honour, get honest.

Q. Why is the Devil always a gentleman?
A. Because he's the imp o' darkness, so he can't be imp o' light.

Q. How do we know that Moses wore a wig?
A. Because he was sometimes seen with Aaron, and sometimes without.

Q. Why didn't the worms go into the ark in pairs?
A. They went in apples

THERE'S SOMETHING FISHY GOING ON HERE!

Q. What do fish do when they are hard up?

A.
Kippers give up smoking at once; the *flat fish* move into one room because it's cheaper; the *trout* turn off the current to save electricity, and the *electric eel* switches itself off; the *mussels* relax on the river bed, so that they don't have to shell out any more cash: the *oysters* sell their pearls to earls and make a good penny out of it; the *mackerel* get free lunch at their schools; *salmon* go to any river Bank that's open, but the fish in the Thames only go to the Westminster Bank; the tiny fish go to see their friend Min, because *minnows* them money, and it's no good going to ask a *clam* for anything because he's darned *shellfish* anyway; the *cod* sends itself by post (C.O.D.) and collects the cash when it gets there; *tadpoles* go to a frog-spawnbroker; *goldfish* don't have a thing to worry about; the *whiting* whites a cheque; *mullet* are used to being in the red, so they just mull it over, and wait for the tide to turn; the *shark* eats a millionaire for breakfast and coughs up the cash; the *sole* is the only one who does not give a damn because it's quite above money troubles and who ever heard of a sole on its uppers? That's fishy!

SHARPEN YOUR WITS

Q. What is the best thing to take when you are run down by a car?

A. The number.

Q. What kind of doctors do ducks go to?

A. Quack doctors.

Q. Why did the man with an unnatural voice have unnatural teeth?

A. He had a falsetto voice, and a false set o'teeth.

Q. What is the latest thing in dresses?

A. A nightdress.

Q. Why is a worn-out umbrella better than a brand-new one?

A. Because it is most useful when it is used up.

Q. What bird can lift the heaviest weight?

A. The crane.

Q. Why would a compliment from a chicken be an insult?

A. It would be fowl language.

Q. Why is a dog's tail like the heart of a tree?

A. Because it is farthest from the bark.

Q. If a dog loses it's tail, where can he get another?

A. From a retail shop.

Q. Why did the one-handed woman cross the road?

A. To get to the second-hand shop.

Q. Why does a bird with one wing always disagree with a bird with two?

A. Because there is a difference of a pinion between them.

ELEPHANTS

Elephants can live to be as old as 70, but they never forget a riddle (or remember one, for that matter!). Here are some elephants to remember.

Q. What do you use to shoot a purple elephant?
A. A purple elephant gun.

Q. How does an elephant get down from a tree?
A. He sits on a leaf and waits until autumn.

Q. And how do you get down from an elephant?
A. You don't. You get down from a swan (swansdown).

Q. Why is an elephant large, grey and wrinkled?
A. Because if he was small, round and white, he would be an aspirin.

Q. What did the man say when he saw the elephants coming over the hill?
A. Here come the elephants, of course.

Q. What did he say when he saw the elephants coming over the hill with dark glasses on?
A. Nothing. He didn't recognize them.

Q. What's the difference between a sneezing elephant and a spy?
A. No difference at all. They've both got a code in their trunk.

Q. What did the grape say when the elephant stepped on it?
A. Nothing. It just let out a little whine.

Q. Why does an elephant wear ripple-soled shoes?
A. To give the ants a fifty-fifty chance.

Q. What would happen if you crossed an elephant with a kangaroo?
A. There'd be great big holes all over Australia.

Q. But why are elephants grey?
A. So as not to mix them up with strawberries.

Q. But why are they wrinkled?
A. Have you ever tried ironing one?

Q. How do you tell when you're in bed with an elephant?
A. By the big 'E' on his pyjama pocket.

Q. What time is it when an elephant sits on a fence?
A. Time to get a new one.

Q. How do you know you've got an elephant in the fridge?
A. By the hoof-prints in the butter.

BRAIN-TEASERS

Q. What's the name of your tailor?
A. Mr Sew-and-Sew.

Q. What is always at the head of fashion, yet always out of date?
A. The letter F.

Q. Why can there never be a best horse in a race?
A. Because there's always a better.

Q. How can you make a slow horse fast?
A. Tie him up.

Q. When a doctor operates on a dog and comes to his lungs, what does he find?
A. The seat of his pants.

Q. If our peacock laid an egg in your garden, who would own the egg?
A. Nobody. Peahens lay eggs, not peacocks.

Q. Why did they stop putting salt on the roads?
A. Because it was hurting the cats' eyes.

Q. What bird moves in the highest circles?
A. The eagle.

Q. If a boy wears his trousers out, what should he do?
A. Wear them in again, not leave them lying round outside.

Q. What musical key makes a good Army officer?
A. A-sharp major.

Q. What was the jeweller's wife called?
A. Ruby.

> Q. Ten fish I caught without an eye,
> And nine without a tail;
> Six had no head, and half of eight
> I weighed upon the scale.
> Now who can tell me as I ask it,
> How many fish were in my basket?
> A. 0. (10 without an I is 0; 9 without a tail is 0;
> 6 without a head is 0; half of 8 is 0.)

Q. What is it that someone else has to take before you can get it?
A. Your photograph.

Q. What is the surest way to keep water from coming into your house?
A. Never pay the water rate.

Q. Where did Caesar go on his 39th birthday?
A. Into his fortieth year.

Q. What language does an Arabian child speak before it cuts its teeth?
A. Gum Arabic.

ALPHABET RIDDLES

Did you know that an alphabet of only 24 letters can be rearranged in 620,448,410,733,239,439,360,000 different ways? No wonder there are one or two alphabet riddles!

1. These letters were written on the communion table of a small church in Wales and went on puzzling the congregation for many centuries. What could they mean? By adding only *one* vowel, but as many times as you like, can you manage to make sense of it?

P R S V R Y P R F C T M N
V R K P T H S P R C P T S T N

2. How can you say, 'I'm looking for you,' in 3 letters?

3. What word of six letters means exactly the opposite by changing the places of the two middle letters?

4. Can you make this out?
>   f the B mt put:
>   f the B. putting:

5. Or this?
>   yy u r
>   yy u b
>   i c u r yy 4 me.

6. What was this man doing?
    Captain BBBB and his CCCC went to the DWD.

7. Which two English words contain all the vowels of the alphabet *in the right order*?

8. What is this flower?

> Inscribe an m above a line
> And write an e below.
> This woodland flower is hung so fine,
> It sways when breezes blow.

9. And who is this?

> With letters three indite my name,
> Add one to show what I became,
> Two more to tell what brought me fame.

10. What are the two words described here?

> Eight letters, (start with B),
> Three syllables contain;
> Take one away and see,
> Four syllables remain.

11. This poem spells out a word. What is it?

> My first is in saddle and also in strap,
> My second's in programme and also in map,
> My third is in letter and also in send,
> My fourth is in tearing and also in rend,
> My fifth is in linden and also in lime,
> My sixth is in clamber and also in climb,
> My seventh's in clatter and also in roar,
> My whole is a land great in peace and war.

12. And here is another.

> My first is in people but not in crowd,
> My second's in shower but not in cloud,
> My third is in apple but not in pie,
> My fourth is in purchase but not in buy,
> My fifth is in Peter but not in Paul,
> My whole is a state desired by all.

13.   My first is a circle, my second a cross,
      If you meet my whole, look for a toss.

14. Can you make out this word? It begins with a T and is
spelled in capital letters.

                Make three-fourths of a cross,
                    And let a circle complete:
                And let two semicircles
                    On a perpendicular meet;
                Next add a triangle
                    That stands on two feet;
                Next two semicircles,
                    And a circle complete.

15.   Thomas a Tattatamus took two T's,
      To tie two tups to two tall trees.
      To frighten the terrible Thomas a Tattamus,
      How many T's are there in all that?

Answers: 1. Persevere ye perfect men. Ever keep these
precepts ten. 2. ICQ. 3. United and Untied. 4. If the
grate be empty put coal on. If the grate be full, stop putting
coal on. 5. Too wise you are, too wise you be. I see you
are too wise for me. 6. Captain Forbes and his forces went
to the West Indies. 7. Facetious and abstemious. 8.
Anemone. 9. Poe, poet, Poetry. 10. Beautify, and beatify.
11. America. 12. Peace. 13. Ox. 14. TOBACCO.
15. 2.

Q. What is the best system of book-keeping?
A. Never lend them.

Q. A woman had a son who lived in Doncaster, who was always wiring for money. Why didn't she mind?
A. He was an electrician.

Q. Why did the woodman spare the tree?
A. He was a good feller.

Q. What herb cures all things?
A. Thyme.

Q. Why is it dangerous to put a clock at the top of the stairs?
A. Because it might run down and strike one.

Q. What makes pies inquisitive?
A. S will make spies of them.

Q. Why is an old loaf like a mouse running into a hole?
A. Because you can see it's stale (its tail).

Q. How is it that a horse has six legs?
A. He has forelegs in front and two legs behind.

Q. Why is tennis such a noisy game?
A. Because every player raises a racket.

Q. What are the best tunes?
A. Fortunes – made up of bank-notes.

Q. What time is it when you see a monkey scratching with his left hand?
A. Five after one.

MONKEY-TRICKS

Q. Why did the monkey make his bed high up in the chandelier?

A. He was a light sleeper.

Q. How did the monkey burgle the ice-cream van?

A. Jumped on to the roof, and got them to hand up the lolly.

Q. How do you catch a monkey?

A. Hang upside down in a tree and make a noise like a banana.

Q. A monkey who was locked up in a room with a piano, managed to escape, even though there weren't any windows. How?

A. He played the piano until he found the right key.

Q. Why did the monkey hide up the tree?

A. Because he had a bear behind.

QUESTIONS, QUESTIONS!

Q. I haven't got it, don't want it, wouldn't have it. But if I had it, I would not part with it for the whole world. What is it?

A. A bald head.

Q. In the night a mountain, in the morning a meadow. What is it?

A. A bed.

A tea-kettle is a tea-kettle,
A tea-kettle has what everything has,
Now what has a tea-kettle?
A. A name.

Q. What is it that goes out black, and comes in white?

A. A black cow on a snowy day.

Q. If two is company and three is a crowd, what are four and five?

A. Nine.

Q. Why should you never believe the word of a Dutchman?

A. Because Holland is such a low-lying country.

Q. What's the most important use for cowhide?

A. To hold the cow together.

Q. Who was the most popular actor in the Bible?

A. Samson; because he brought the house down.

Q. What did the rebel read at University?

A. The riot act.

Q. Why can't you ever have a whole day's holiday?
A. Because day breaks at the beginning.

Q. What island is six-sided?
A. Cuba.

Q. Why is playing chess better than playing whist?
A. Because you play chess with two bishops but whist with four knaves.

Q. What four letters frighten a thief?
A. O I C U.

Q. What long word has only one letter in it?
A. An envelope.

Q. Who is given the sack as soon as he starts work?
A. A postman.

Q. Why does a miller wear a white hat?
A. To keep his head warm.

Q. Why does a bear wear a fur coat?
A. Because it would look ridiculous in a mackintosh.

Q. Which is the left side of a pudding?
A. The side which isn't eaten.

Q. How many eggs can a giant eat on an empty stomach?
A. One.

Q. How many hairs are there in a cat's tail?
A. None. They are all on the outside.

Q. What's the best way to make a clean sweep?
A. Wash him.

Q. How would you make a Maltese Cross with one match?
A. Strike it and stick it up his sweater.

Q. There were two Bishops in bed. Which one wore the nightie?
A. Mrs Bishop.

Q. The more you take, the more you leave behind. What are they?
A. Footsteps.

Q. What tea-pot can you never get a cup of tea from?
A. An empty one.

Q. What is Australia bounded by?
A. Kangaroos.

Q. Why is a bigamist like the captain of a ship?
A. Because he has a second mate.

Q. If a waiter were carrying a turkey on a dish, and let it fall, what three great national calamities would occur?
A. The downfall of Turkey, the breaking up of China, and the overthrow of Greece.

Q. Why does it take 50 nitwits to put a screw in a wall?
A. Because it takes one to hold the screw, one to hold the screwdriver, and 48 to turn the wall.

ROOM FOR IMPROVEMENT

Q. There's a man in a room, without doors or windows. The only furniture is a wooden table. How does the man get out?

A. First of all he bangs his head against the wall until it's sore. He takes the saw and cuts the table in half. He puts the two halves together to make a whole. He gets through the hole, and then he shouts and shouts until he's hoarse. He gets on the horse and rides away.

Q. Why is a room packed with married people like an empty room?

A. Because there is not a single person in it!

> A little house full of meat,
> No door to go in and eat.
> A. A nut.

Q. What's a house with one leg?

A. An umbrella.

Q. If you were locked in a room with only a bed and a calendar, how could you survive?

A. You could drink water from the springs of the bed, and eat dates from the calendar.

Q. What did the man do when he thought he was dying?

A. Moved into the living-room.

Q. What is the most striking thing you can have in a room?

A. A grandfather clock.

Q. What did the chimney and door do when the room caught on fire?

A. The chimney flue and the door bolted.

Q. There were two men, once, shut up in a room without anything to eat, and yet though the room was completely empty, they both managed to survive. How was that?

A. One man bolted the door. Then he told his friend a very tall story, and his friend swallowed it whole.

Q. How can you get out of a room with a locked door and no windows? (You have got a piece of chalk in your pocket.)

A. You make a cross on the door, with the chalk, and so you exit (X it).

> In marble walls as white as milk,
> Lined with a skin as soft as silk;
> Within a fountain crystal clear,
> A golden apple does appear.
> No doors there are to this stronghold,
> Yet thieves break in and steal the gold.
> A. ·ᵷᵷə u∀

HOW'S THAT AGAIN?

Q. Why did the penny stamp?
A. Because the threepenny bit.

Q. Why did the lobster blush?
A. Someone shut it up in the fridge with salad dressing.

Q. Can the orange box?
A. No. But the tomato can.

Q. Why was the ghost turned out of the pub at midnight?
A. Because they don't serve spirits after hours.

Q. How can you buy a dog going cheap?
A. You can't. That's birds. Dogs go woof-woof.

> Patch upon patch,
> Without any stitches,
> If you tell me this riddle,
> I'll give you my breeches!
> A. A cabbage.

Q. What did the irate circus owner say to the stubborn elephant?
A. Pack your trunk and get out.

Q. What did the big firework say to the little firework?
A. My pop is bigger than your pop.

Q. What goes up when the rain comes down?
A. An umbrella.

Two black-white doves
Who reach the skies,
Yet keep their nests,
For they are . . .
A. Eyes.

Q. What kind of animal can jump higher than a house?
A. All kinds. Houses can't jump.

Q. What is a bird after he is four days old?
A. Five days old.

Q. What is the first thing you put in a garden?
A. Your foot.

Q. What did the earwig say when it fell off the wall?
A. 'Ere we go.

Q. What did the chicken say when it came out of the egg?
A. Marmalade. (Ma me laid.)

Q. What did the bull say when it swallowed the bomb?
A. Abominable.

Q. What animal is the opposite of a yes-man?
A. A no-bull.

Q. What did Noah say when he heard the rain come down?
A. 'Ark!

Q. What water never freezes?
A. Hot water.

Q. What is most like a horse but isn't a horse?
A. A mare.

Q. What goes up but never comes down?
A. Your age.

Q. What has four legs and can fly?
A. Two birds.

Q. What has six eyes and cannot see?
A. Three blind mice.

Q. What goes up a tree with its head turned downwards?
A. A nail in your shoe.

Q. What does your mother look for and hope not to find?
A. A hole in your sock.

Q. Riddle me, riddle me, riddle me ree,
   I saw a nutcracker up in a tree. What was that?
A. A squirrel.

Q. What has a neck but cannot swallow?
A. A bottle.

Q. What's the dirtiest thing in the house?
A. The clock, because it has hands but never washes its face.

Q. When is a sailor not a sailor?
A. When he's aboard.

Q. Why isn't it safe to sleep in trains?
A. Because trains run over sleepers.

Q. What gets wetter the more it dries?
A. A towel.

Q. What is black and white and red all over?
A. A newspaper.

> Runs over fields and woods all day,
> Under the bed at night sits not alone,
> With long tongue hanging out,
> A-waiting for a bone.
> A. Shoe.

Q. What grows bigger the more you take from it?
A. A hole.

Q. What is in the middle of Paris?
A. R.

Q. Who died but was not born?
A. Adam.

Q. Why did Cain kill his brother?
A. Because he was able.

Q. Drawers without handles?
A. Knickers.

> A skin have I,
> More eyes than one.
> I can be nice when I am done.
> A. Potato.

Q. What digs coal and is quite small?
A. A mini-miner.

Q. Which King of France wore the biggest shoes?
A. The one with the biggest feet.

Q. What do baby apes sleep in?
A. Apricots.

Q. What is copper nitrate?
A. Overtime for policemen.

Q. When is a tap not a tap?
A. When it is dripping.

Q. Why did the coal scuttle?
A. Because it saw the kitchen sink.

Q. Who wrote, 'Thoughts of a Chinese Cat'?
A. Miao Tse-tung.

Q. What do you get when you cross a mink with a stoat?
A. Moat stoles and stink coats.

Q. What two French towns are like a sailor's trousers?
A. Toulon and Toulouse.

Q. What comes steaming and splashing out of Cowes?
A. The Royal Yacht.

Q. What should you do if you are hungry?
A. Run around the park until you get fed up.

Q. Eight watches were stolen from a jeweller's. Who were the police looking for?
A. A punctual octopus.

Q. What does a cashier in a police-station do?
A. He counts the coppers.

Q. How did the Vikings send secret messages?
A. By Norse code.

Q. How do you make a German jump?
A. Shout 'Hans up'.

Q. How do you catch a chicken?
A. Put a pox on it.

Q. A machine was invented in England, made in Italy, then sent to Poland. What happened to it there?
A. It was Warsaw Pact.

Q. If Cromwell's men were roundheads, what are Russia's women?
A. Redheads.

Q. If a man who comes third is good, and the second is better, who is best?
A. A footballer.

Q. How would it be if both our feet were on one leg?
A. An amazing feat!

Q. What is even harder in life than taking things as they come?
A. Parting with things as they go.

Q. If an apple-tree has five branches, and on each branch 30 leaves in May, and it grows 1 leaf a month, how many leaves will it have in 8 months' time?
A. None.

Q. What's black and white and black and white and black and white?

A. A nun rolling down a hill with a penguin in her arms.

Q. What's black and white and red all over?

A. A sunburnt penguin.

Q. Why don't elephants like penguins?

A. They can't get the paper off with their trunks.

Q. What food gives you an electric shock?

A. A currant bun.

Q. Why was the baker so rude?

A. He was badly bred.

Q. What can be long and short, and wet and dry, and green and black?

A. A spring.

Q. What's the noisiest season?

A. Rusty spring.

Q. What's yellow and stupid?

A. Thick custard.

Q. What's the fastest type of string in the world?

A. Con-cord.

Q. Why was the famous musician struck by lightning?

A. He was a good conductor.

Q. Why did William Tell?

A. Because the banana split.

Q. When is ink like a sheep?

A. When it's in a pen.

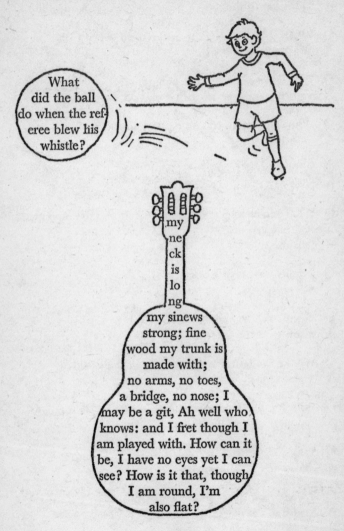

54

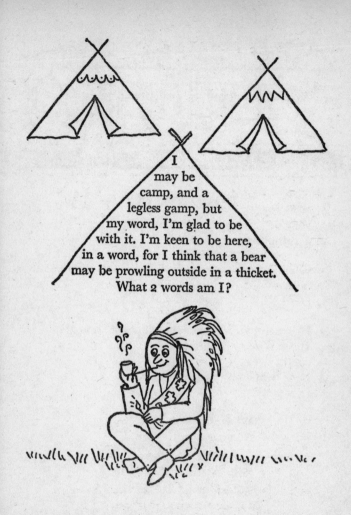

I may be camp, and a legless gamp, but my word, I'm glad to be with it. I'm keen to be here, in a word, for I think that a bear may be prowling outside in a thicket. What 2 words am I?

Answers: He looked round. The guitar can C sharp and B flat. Content and intent.

GOOD TRAINING

Q. Why do trains never run on time?
A. Because they run on rails.

Q. What did the man say when he fell off the railway bridge?
A. Hard lines.

Q. How can you tell when an old engine is angry?
A. When it gets all steamed up.

Q. How does a fast train speak?
A. It expresses itself.

> What goes with a train,
> And comes with a train,
> And the train doesn't need it,
> But can't go without it?
> A. Noise.

Q. Do you think trains are contented with their way of life?
A. Yes, they never try to rise above their station.

Q. What goes whistling up the aisle at a wedding?
A. The bride's train.

Q. What did the station master?
A. Reading between the lines.

Q. What is the difference between a train and an Atlantic rower?
A. One goes on the rails, and the other rows in the gales.

Q. Why does the goods train need no engine?
A. Because the goods make the cargo.

Q. Why should you never complain about the price of a railway ticket?
A. It's bound to be fare.

Q. What motive did the inventor of railways have?
A. A locomotive.

Q. What's this – only two backbones, but a thousand ribs?
A. Railway track.

Q. What runs all the way from Carlisle to London without moving?
A. A railway line.

Q. At which station can you use the lavatory, when the train is standing still?
A. Waterloo.

Q. What became of the man who had a funny accident?
A. He was in stitches.

Q. What's a quick snack for a cannibal?
A. A sandwich-man.

Q. What did the undertaker die of?
A. Coffin'.

Q. How does a bookmaker behave?
A. He makes himself a tome.

Q. What makes more noise than a pig stuck under a gate?
A. Two pigs stuck under a gate.

Q. What girl knows all about explosions?
A. Dinah Mite.

Q. Who works with a will?
A. A lawyer.

Q. When does a soldier go to pieces?
A. When he's in quarters.

Q. Why does a horse talk with his mouth full?
A. He always has a bit in his mouth.

Q. What turns without moving?
A. Milk.

Q. What is the principal part of a horse?
A. The mane part.

Q. How can you take two letters away from a four-letter word and have four left?
A. Take F and E from FIVE, leaving IV.

Q. Why did the window box?
A. Because it saw the garden fence.

Q. What's the most athletic vegetable?
A. A runner bean.

Q. What's green and jumps around the garden?
A. A spring cabbage.

Q. Why was the billiard-player late?
A. He missed his cue.

Q. Is smoking always harmful?
A. No. It can cure kippers.

Q. What must you always fight to get?
A. A black eye.

Q. If a swan sings a swan song, what does a cygnet sing?
A. A signature tune.

Q. Why is a spectator like a beehive?
A. Because a spectator is a beholder; and a bee-holder is a beehive.

BACK SLANG

Ancay ouyay underyayandstay isthay?

(All the answers include the name of a country.)

Onceyay uponyay ayay imetay erethay asway ayay ittlelay irlgay. Atwhay asway erhay amenay?
Icilysay.

Isthay ittlelay irlgay asway rightfayullyfay inthay. Atwhay ountrycay idday eshay ivelay inyay?
Inlandfay.

Erhay othermay awsay erhay yingcray. Atwhay idday ethay othermay aysay?
'Areyay ouyay ungaryhay?'

Atwhay idday ethay ildchay answeryay?
'Esyay, iamsay.'

Atwhay idday Icilysay askyay erhay othermay enthay?
'Enyakay ivegay emay omesayingthay otay eatyay?'

Atwhay idday ethay othermay ivegay erhay otay eatyay?
Ayay licesay ofyay urkeytay.

Utbay Icilysay artedstay otay ycray againyay. Ywhay asway atthay?
Eshay antedway amoasay.

60

Atwhay idday ethay othermay aysay isthay imetay?
'Ohyay, orfay oodgayessnay akesay, opstay osethay
aleshway.'

Andyay enwhay Icilysay illstay entway onyay akingmay
ayay astynay oisenay, atwhay idday erhay othermay aysay?
'Enmarkday ymay ordsway. Oday asyay ouyay areyay
oldtay, oryay Iyay illway ivegay ouyay ayay anzaniatay?'

'Atwhay isyay ATTHAY?'

Icilysay idday otnay aitway otay indfay outyay. Atwhay
idday eshay aysay?
'Iranyay awayyay.'

(The answers are at the back of the book.)

SMILES AND SMIRKS

Q. How do you join the Army?
A. Handcuff them together.

Q. What sits on the bottom of the sea, singing, 'Give me
the moonlight'?
A. Frankie Praughan.

Q. Why do you go over a hill?
A. Because you can't go under it.

Q. Why can't a skeleton jump off a cliff?
A. He hasn't got any guts.

Q. What collects money but never spends it?
A. A money-box.

Q. Why aren't monkeys well-paid?
A. Because they only get peanuts.

Q. What jumps out of the ground shouting, 'knickers, knickers'?
A. Crude oil.

Q. And what jumps out of the ground shouting 'underwear, underwear'?
A. Refined oil.

Q. Why is it a good idea to have holes in your trousers?
A. To put your feet through.

Q. What sleeps at the bottom of the sea?
A. A kipper.

Q. What is the difference between a tiny witch and an escaping deer?
A. One is a stunted hag, the other is a hunted stag.

Q. What did the cat burglar say when he was caught?
A. Me-ow!

Q. Who invented the sword dance?
A. Someone who wanted to enjoy himself and cut his toe-nails at the same time.

Q. What does a Scotsman have for pudding?
A. Tart-an pie.

REVERSE RIDDLES

The answer is – what is the question?

A. Fish fingers.
Q. Supposing your legs suddenly disappear and you grow a long scaly tail; then your arms shrivel up and turn into fins; then all your hair drops out; what can you count on next?

A. Nine W.

Q. 'Mr Wagner, is your name spelt with a "V"?' (nine=nein=no).

A. Ashes.

Q. If a ton of coal costs £12, and a ton of anthracite works out at £14, what does a load of firewood come to?

A. Climate.

Q. If you can't go round a mountain, what do you do?

A. FGHIJKLMNOPQRSTUVWXY.

Q. What's the difference between an E-type and a Z car?

A. Guerilla warfare, sir.

Q. 'I say, chaps, do you mind awfully putting down those bananas, and coming down from the trees. Right. Now what in God's name are you up to?'

A. BLND PG

Q. How do you spell blind pig?

A. Office desk.

Q. A man took a train to town on Monday morning, walked to the City, went calmly into his office, then suddenly leaped into the air and took a running jump towards the window. Where did he go then?

A. A bridge.

Q. If God made light and darkness on the first day; Heaven on the second day; earth and sea on the third; what did He make on the Forth?

Q. What did the man say when he staggered into the Queen's Arms?

A. You shouldn't have bothered, your Majesty.

Q. What did the man say when St Peter sent him down to Hell?

A. I'm damned if I'm going there!

Q. How did the angry engineer make a reservoir?

A. He sent the hillside to blazes, blew up the rocks, blasted the river bed, and then damned the river.

Q. Who eats Queen of puddings?

A. A communist cannibal.

Q. What does St Michael do in Heaven?

A. Makes clothes.

Q. What kind of hat can play a tune?

A. A hat with a band on it.

Q. What did Big Chief Running Water call his two sons?
A. Hot and Cold.

Q. And what did he call his third son?
A. Little Drip.

Q. What men shave twenty times a day?
A. Barbers.

Q. Why is a policeman the strongest man in the world?
A. Because he can stop a 10-ton truck with one hand.

Q. If a boy should lose a knee, where would he go for another?
A. To the butcher, where kid-neys are sold.

Q. What is the best way to make trousers last?
A. Make the coat first.

Q. Why is it a mistake to wear a bedroom slipper?
A. Because when you do, you put your foot in it.

Q. How can you make a pearl out of a pear?
A. Add L.

Q. What are the little white things in your head that bite?
A. Teeth.

Q. Why should an owl be offended if you called him a pheasant?
A. You'd be making game of him.

Q. Why is a poultry-dealer like a bank robber?
A. They both make their money by foul means.

RHYMING SLANG

It's not likely you'd hear anyone using all these words, because they are a mixture of rhyming slangs – Cockney, theatrical, Irish, American, Army. And they go in and out of fashion too (like fab, and gear, and groovy). I've just put them in here for the fun of the thing. I wonder if you can make out what's going on in the story on page 68?

Stairs	apples and pears.
Bottle	Aristotle – 'Arry Stottle.
Legs	bacon and eggs – fried eggs, clothes pegs.
Soap	Band of Hope – Cape of Good Hope.
Money	bees and honey
	sugar and honey = sugar.
Wife	bit of tripe, carving-knife, trouble and strife.
Night	black and white.
Face	boat race.
Old hag	boiled rag.
Sleep	bo-peep.
Watch	bottle of scotch.
Police	copper, bottle and stopper, grasshopper.
Sneeze	bread and cheese.
Coat	bucket and float.
Row	bull and cow.
Knees	bugs and fleas.
Look	butcher's hook = butcher's.
Neck	bushel and peck.
House	cat and mouse.
Bike	clever mike.
Laugh	cow and calf.
Head	crust of bread, loaf of bread = loaf.

Boots	daisy roots.
Bombs	Derry and Toms.
Moustache	dot and dash.
Dook	Duke of York(s) = forks = fingers = fists.
Mouth	north and south.
Drunk	elephant's trunk.
Street	field of wheat.
Water	fisherman's daughter.
Sight	flash o'light.
Road	frog and toad.
Pardon	garden.
Morning	gypsy's warning.
Kids	God forbids.
Chin	Gunga Din.
Liar	holy friar.
Man	geezer, ice-cream freezer.
Crook	Joe Rook.
Trousers	jolly rousers.
Car	la-di-dah.
Fingers	long and lingers.
Pound	lost and found.
Knife	man and wife.
Cupboard	Mother Hubbard.
Eyes	mince-pies.
Ghost	pillar and post.
Feet	plates of meat = plates.
Talk	rabbit and pork.
Supper	Tommy Tucker.
River	shake and shiver.
Butter	stammer and stutter.
Train	struggle and strain.
Telephone	switch and bone.
Thieving	tea-leafing.
Late	tiddler's bait.
Drink	tiddly wink.

Hat	tit for tat = titfer.
Dirty	two-thirty.
Bed	Uncle Ned.
Boy	pride and joy.
Girl	ivory-pearl.
Ball o'chalk	walk.
Window	winder, burnt cinder.

'Look at that dickory dock. Up them apples and pears, into Uncle Ned.'

TEA-LEAFING DOWN THE FROG AND TOAD

There was this bloke, see, with his trouble an' strife. I wus on me clever mike ridin' down the field of wheat, an' I got a butcher's at 'em. The bloke had a titfer an' a dot an' dash, an' they was bof goin' for a ball-o'chalk, mindin' their own business. Or was they?

But then, what does this geezer do, but slip 'is long and lingers in the jolly rousers of the old ice-cream freezer in front of 'im. Looks like a bit of tea-leafing, I finks.

So I stops. There ain't no bottle and stopper. Just these two Joe Rooks, havin' a rabbit an' pork. But the first geezer I see, the one with the titfer an' the dot an' dash, he's shoving some bees and honey belongin' to the old freezer right into 'is pocket!

So I steps up smart, and says, 'Beg yer garden,' and I puts me plates down 'ard on 'is daisy roots.

You should've seen 'is boat race! 'Is north and south twists up something terrible, and he gives me such a blooming butcher's outer 'is mince-pies. So I ups with me bacon and eggs into his bugs and fleas, throws a dook into his Gunga Din, and there 'e is, flat on 'is flaming back in the frog and toad.

Up comes a grasshopper, out of nowhere. The boiled rag, that's the geezer's carving-knife, is doing 'er nut!

Screamin' and shoutin'. 'Ere, ere, ere,' says the grasshopper, and gets me by the bushel and peck. What a bull an' cow! A cow an' calf, if youse asks me.

Then, what does this holy friar do, but picks isself up, all two-thirty an' 'is loaf a flash o'light, and sez I'm tryin' to nick 'is bottle of scotch! An' then if 'is bit of tripe doesn't chip in too, and there's another bull an' cow startin' up.

So what does I do? I finks it's time to scarper. So I does. I shakes the copper's dooks off of me peck, nicks a lost and found outer the Rook's bucket and float, and jumps on me mike.

But I gets meself a smashing Tommy Tucker outer that geezer's sugar. Alligator.

And blimey, if I don't see the very same geezer next gypsy's warnin', drivin' 'is la-di-dah down the frog and toad. And, blimey, if I don't find out 'is cat and mouse.

An' den a very funny fing 'appens. Wouldjer believe it, if the very next black an' white, a 'Arry Stottle doesn't go clean frew one of the burnt cinders of that very cat and mouse? – accidental like.

HAPPY DAYS

Q. How can you take six away from a King of Israel, and leave his father?
A. Take VI from DAVID, and leave DAD.

Q. What is most like a cat looking in at a window?
A. A cat looking in at a window.

Q. When is it perfectly polite to serve milk in a saucer?
A. When you're feeding the cat.

Q. What man must have a glass or two before starting work?
A. A glazier.

Q. Why should a naval officer never put his chronometer under his pillow?
A. Because he should never sleep on his watch.

Q. How can you stop a cock crowing at dawn on Monday?
A. Eat him for Sunday dinner.

Q. At what time of day was Adam born?
A. A little before Eve.

Q. Why did Adam bite the apple?
A. Because he hadn't got a knife.

Q. How was Moses cured?
A. The Lord gave him two tablets.

Q. What does a diamond become when it is placed in water?
A. Wet.

DANGER! MEN AT WORK

Some people manage to make a good thing out of their work . . .

What did the manufacturer of cardboard make?
A packet.

What did the inventor of carpets make?
A pile.

What did the astrologer make?
A fortune.

What did the inventor of copying machines make?
A million.

What did Marco Polo make?
A mint.

What did the inventor of engraving make?
A pretty penny.

> As I went over Heepo Steeple,
> I met up with a heap o' people,
> Some was nicky, some was nacky,
> Some was the colour o' brown tobacky.
> A. Anthill of ants.

Q. Why was the lift-attendant depressed?
A. Because his job got him down.

Q. Why did the carpenter give up his work?
A. Because he was always getting board, and having a raw deal.

Q. Why was the bill-poster sacked?
A. Because he couldn't stick at the job.

Q. How did the shoemaker die?
A. He coughed his last.

> Two brothers we are,
>   Great burdens we bear,
> All day we are bitterly pressed;
>   Yet this I will say –
>   We are full all the day,
> And empty when we go to rest.
> A. Shoes.

Q. Why did the cleaner stop cleaning?
A. Because she found grime doesn't pay.

GIGGLES AND GROANS

Q. Two biscuits were crossing the road, when one was run over. What did the other say?
A. Oh, crumbs!

Q. If slippers are slippers, and shoes are shoes, what are boots?
A. Chemists.

Q. What did the carpet say to the table?
A. I can see your drawers.

Q. There were 3 tomatoes racing across the desert. Which one was the cowboy?
A. None. They were all redskins.

Q. Why does the giraffe have such a long neck?
A. So his head can reach his body.

Q. What goes over the water, under the water and on the water, and yet does not touch the water?
A. An egg in a duck's tummy.

Q. Can a man marry his widow's sister?
A. No, because he'd be dead.

Q. What is brown and sounds like a bell?
A. Dung.

Q. Why do elephants jump out of trees at 3 o'clock in the morning?
A. Because they're practising parachute jumping.

Q. Why did the one-eyed bird walk across the road?
A. To get to the bird's eye shop.

Q. Why did the orange stop rolling down the hill?
A. Because he ran out of juice.

Q. What's the best time to pick an apple?
A. When the farmer is asleep.

Q. When is a boy not a boy?
A. When he's a little pale.

Q. What did the big candle say to the little candle?
A. I'm going out tonight.

Q. How many relatives depend on you for a living?
A. Your uncles, aunts and cousins, because without U they could not exist.

CRAZY CATS

Q. What's a copy-cat?
A· An artist painting a self-portrait.

Q. What animal goes hunting mice in the sea?
A. A catfish.

Q. Where do cats get their money?
A. From the catmint.

Q. What paper does a cat read on Sunday?
A. The Mews of the World.

Q. What's the weather like when you meet a mouse carrying an umbrella?

A. Raining cats and dogs.

Q. How does a cat feel when he's cleared all the mice out of the house?

A. Mouse proud.

Q. Where do catfish carry their money when they go shopping?

A. In a paw purse (porpoise).

Q. What's cataarh?

A. The sound a cat makes when a doctor looks down its throat.

MADDER AND MADDER

Q. Can you drop a full glass without spilling any water?
A. Yes, if the glass is full of milk.

Q. What bird can't fly as high as you can jump?
A. A bird in a cage.

Q. Why can't ducks fly upside down?
A. Because they would quack up.

Q. What did the police frog say to the naughty frog?
A. Go on, hop it.

Q. What is a cat's favourite holiday resort?
A. The Canary Islands.

Q. Do restaurants serve crabs?
A. Yes. If they sit down.

Q. What do you call an Eskimo with 12 balaclava helmets on?
A. You can call him anything because he won't hear you.

Q. If you were walking along a street without any trousers on and you saw a copper, what should you do?
A. Pick it up.

Q. Why did the cashier steal money out of the till?
A. She thought the change would do her good.

Q. Why was the man disqualified in the Transatlantic Singlehanded Race?
A. He used both hands.

Q. A man went swimming, and while he was in the water, all his clothes were stolen. What did he come home in?
A. The dark.

Q. Why is it hard to believe that the Blarney Stone is genuine?
A. Because there are so many shamrocks in Ireland.

Q. What is worse than raining cats and dogs?
A. Hailing taxis when it's raining cats and dogs as well.

Q. When did the waiter stop waiting?
A. When he got his just desserts.

Q. How can you write a composition, using only two letters?
A. Write an SA.

WHAT'S THE DIFFERENCE?

Q. What's the difference between an oak tree and a tight shoe?
A. One makes acorns, and the other makes corns ache.

Q. What's the difference between a penniless man and a feather bed?
A. One is hard up, and the other is soft down.

Q. What's the difference between an extra policeman and an England footballer?
A. One more bobby – and one Bobby Moore!

Q. What's the difference between a letter in the post and a woman going along the road?
A. One is addressed in an envelope and the other is enveloped in a dress.

Q. What's the difference between an angry circus owner and a Roman barber?
A. One is a raving showman and the other is a shaving Roman.

Q. What's the difference between a thought, a sigh, a mink coat, and a monkey?
A. A thought is an idea, a sigh is 'Oh dear!', a mink coat is too dear, and a monkey is *you*, dear.

Q. What's the difference between a glass of water and a glass of whisky?
A. About 50p.

Q. What's the difference between a rotten husband and a rotten shot?
A. One hits his missus, and the other misses his hits.

Q. What's the difference between a gold-miner and a drunkard?
A. One turns his gold into quarts, and the other turns his quartz into gold.

Q. What's the difference between a cow and a broken chair?
A. One gives milk, and the other gives way (whey).

Q. What's the difference between a cat and a comma?
A. One has its claws at the end of its paws, and the other a pause at the end of its clause.

Q. What's the difference between a summer dress in winter, and an extracted tooth?
A. One is too thin, and the other is tooth out.

Q. What's the difference between a riddle and some children sitting on a bun?
A. One is a conundrum, and the other is a bun under 'em.

Q. What's the difference between a thief and a church bell?
A. One peals from the steeple, and the other steals from the people.

Q. What's the difference between a gossip and a mirror?
A. One speaks without reflecting and the other reflects without speaking.

Q. What's the difference between a schoolboy studying and a farmer watching his cattle?
A. One is stocking his mind and the other is minding his stock.

Q. What's the difference between a drainpipe and a stupid Dutchman?
A. One is a hollow cylinder, the other is a silly Hollander.

Q. What's the difference between Prince Charles and water in a fountain?
A. One is heir to the throne, and the other is thrown to the air.

Q. What's the difference between a tree and an aeroplane?
A. A tree sheds its leaves, while an aeroplane leaves its shed.

Q. What's the difference between a copying-machine and the flu?
A. One makes facsimiles, and the other makes sick families.

Q. What's the difference between a jeweller and a jailor?
A. One sells watches, and the other watches cells.

Q. What's the difference between an auction and sea sickness?
A. One is the sale of effects, and the other the effects of a sail.

Q. What's the difference between a cup of tea and a magician?
A. One is a cuppa, and the other is a sorcerer.

Q. What did the carpet say to the floor?
A. Don't move, I've got you covered.

Q. What is the best way to remove paint?
A. Sit down on it before it is dry.

> The Queen of Morocco,
> She wrote to the King,
> For a bottomless vessel,
> To put flesh and blood in.
> A. ·ɓuıɹ ∀

Q. If you woke up in the night, what would you do for a light?
A. Take a feather from the pillow; that's light enough.

Q. Why is Buckingham Palace the cheapest palace ever built?
A. Because it was built for one sovereign, and furnished for another.

Q. Is there any difference between the North and South Pole?
A. All the difference in the world!

Q. Can you possibly explain this? There were two boys who were born in March: their birthday was in September; and they married each other!
A. The boys were born in the town of March in Cambridgeshire. They were born in the month of September. They both became clergymen and each performed the marriage service for the other.

Q. A man was lying in the road, after having been knocked down by a car. Up came a policeman, and bending over the man, said, 'Have an accident, sir?' What did the man reply?

A. 'No thanks, I've had one already.'

Q. What is invisible – has four feet and a tail – and makes you scream in the dark?

A. A nightmare.

Q. What did the workmen say to the foreman, when they'd finished building the A3?

A. Major road, sir.

Q. For what man should you always take your hat off?

A. A barber.

Q. What is white, has just one horn, and gives milk?

A. A milk truck.

Q. What kind of animal eats with its tail?

A. All kinds of animals eat with their tails, because they can't take them off.

Q. What did the mother sardine say to her baby when they saw a submarine?

A. Don't be afraid. Its only a tin of people.

Q. How do you keep cool at a football match?

A. Sit next to a fan.

Q. What was the elephant doing on the M1?

A. About two miles an hour.

Q. Who invented the sewing machine?

A. Some clever so and so.

Q. Why is 'G' like the sun?
A. Because it's the centre of light.

Q. Why will television never take the place of newspapers?
A. Have you ever tried swatting flies with a television?

Q. Why is there a mother's day, a father's day, but not a son's day?
A. But there is a Sunday every week.

Q. Why did the boy swallow 10p?
A. Because it was his dinner money.

Q. How far can a pirate ship go?
A. Fifteen miles to the galleon.

Q. Is gas made from wood?
A. Yes. Haven't you heard of the Gas Board?

Q. How would you close up the mouth of a river?
A. With a lock and quay.

Q. What do hedgehogs have for dinner?
A. Prickled onions.

Q. Why are bridges annoying?
A. Because they always make you cross.

Q. What did the old man say to a boy who wanted to grow up fast?
A. Grocer.

Q. Why did the boy wear drain-pipe trousers?
A. Because he had water on the knee.

Q. Why did the armless man get killed?
A. As he was 'armless he couldn't shoot back.

Q. What did the new car say to the old car?
A. Do you mean to say you've still got a rattle?

Q. Why did the farmer plough his field with a steam-roller?
A. Because he wanted to raise mashed potatoes.

Q. Why is the letter A like a sweet-smelling flower?
A. Because bee comes after it.

Q. He's in the water and in the air, and though you shoot him, he'll still be there. What is it?
A. Oxygen.

Q. What did the scissors say to the paper?
A. I don't know, but I'm sure it was some cutting remark.

Q. What is the most unsociable thing in the world?
A. A milestone, because you never see two of them together.

Q. What do you go out for and never get?
A. A walk.

Q. How many bricks go to the building of a house?
A. None. They all have to be carried.

Q. Why is wheat like a donkey?
A. Because they both have long ears.

Q. What am I? I've holes through which fingers peep,
        I clash my teeth, but do not weep.
A. Scissors.

WHAT IN THE WORLD?

A riddle, a riddle, as I suppose,
A hundred eyes, and never a nose.
A. A sieve.

I went to the wood and got it;
I sat me down and looked at it;
The more I looked at it the less I liked it;
And I brought it home because I couldn't help it.
A. A thorn.

Q. You can fasten, bolt, lock and bar the house. You can place a watchman on guard continually, and take the keys with you. And yet, before morning, something goes out in spite of you. What is it?
A. The fire in the grate.

Q. What goes upstairs without moving?
A. A carpet.

Q. What stays where it is when it goes off?
A. A gun.

> A house full, a hole full,
> And you cannot gather a bowl full.
> A. Mist.

What shoemaker makes shoes without leather,
With all four elements put together,
> Fire and water, earth and air,
> Every customer has two pair?
A. Blacksmith.

> You use it between your head and toes,
> The more it works the thinner it grows.
> A. Bar of soap.

> What is it?
> Got a mouth, and don't speak,
> Got a bed, and don't sleep?
> A. River.

Q. What has a neck but cannot swallow?
A. A bottle.

Q. What do you like to keep, but find it easy to part with?
A. A comb.

> Q. Twice ten are but six of us,
> Six are but three of us,
> Nine are but four of us,
> What can we possibly be?

> Would you like to know more of us?
> Then I'll tell you more of us.
> Twelve are but six of us,
> Five are but four, do you see?
> A. Letters.

Q. Why ought single girls to stay at home in fine weather?
A. Because they shouldn't have a little son and heir until they are married.

Q. Why are pianos so noble?
A. Because they are upright, grand and square.

Q. Why do people laugh up their sleeves?
A. Because that's where their funnybones are.

Q. Did you ever hear the story of the two holes in the ground?
A. Well, well!

Q. What was the lawyer's wife called?
A. Sue.

Q. What is the best musical motto?
A. B-sharp and B-natural but never B-flat.

Q. What has a head but no hair?
A. A pin.

Q. What has an eye but no head?
A. A needle.

Q. And what has a heart in its head?
A. A cabbage.

Q. What has eight legs, two arms, three heads and wings?
A. A man on horseback, carrying a canary.

Q. What goes up hill and down dale and never moves an inch?
A. A road.

Q. What can water wash, but the sun can't dry?
A. Butter.

Q. Why does a cat sleep much better in summer than in winter?
A. Because the summer brings the cat-er-pillar.

Q. Who's the smallest mother in the world?
A. The minimum.

Q. Why do we sing hymns and not hers?
A. Because we say Amen, and not Awomen.

Q. What fruit travels from pylon to pylon?
A. An electric current.

Q. Why did the fish blush?
A. Because the seaweed.

Q. Why should you take a pencil up to bed with you?
A. To draw the curtains with.

Q. Why did the farmer take a needle into his fields?
A. To sow the corn.

Q. When is a horse not a horse?
A. When it is turned into a stable.

Q. Why is a boxer like a candle?
A. Because a good blow will put them both out.

Q. Why can't you replace my lost canary?
A. Because I wouldn't fit into the cage.

SHAGGY DOGS

Q. What dog keeps the best time?
A. A watch dog.

Q. What did the dying pup say?
A. Well, I'll be doggone.

Q. What's dog-cheap?
A. A cross between a bloodhound and a budgerigar.

Q. How do you find a dog-eared book?
A. Just whistle for it.

Q. What's a sausage dog?
A. A hot dog without the bread.

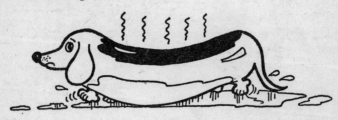

Q. What's a dogma?
A. A mother poodle laying down the law to its pups.
Q. How can you pick dogwood?
A. It's easier with a lead.
Q. Can sleeping dogs lie?
A. They have to. To tell the truth they can't be lying.
Q. When do you have to pay for watcing adog-fight?
A. When they stop fighting each other and turn on you.
Q. And when else?
A. When they are boxers.

Q. What's the tallest race in the world?
A. The steeplechase.

Q. What sea has waves but no water?
A. The BBC.

Q. Why should you always ignore a rhinoceros?
A. Because it doesn't count.

Q. If you have a referee in the game of football, and an umpire in cricket, what do you have in bowls?
A. Goldfish.

Q. Why do we have so many strikes in England?
A. Because of the Union, Jack.

RIDDLE ME REE

Riddle me, riddle me, what is that,
Over the head, and under the hat?
A. ·ɹᴉɐH

Q. Why do we sleep like a log?
A. Because we slumber and it's lumber.

Q. What gets lost every time you stand up?
A. Your lap.

Q. Why is a pilot like special leggings for roadmen?
A. One is a navigator, and the others are navvy gaiters.

Q. What rubbish floats in the Eastern seas?
A. Chinese junk.

Q. Why do birds fly south in the winter time?
A. Because it's too far to walk.

Made in London,
Sold at York,
Stops a bottle,
and is a . . .
A. Cork.

Q. What did the big rose say to the little rose?
A. Hiya, bud.

Q. What did the big goat say to the little goat?
A. You can't kid me.

Q. Why do white sheep eat more grass than black sheep?
A. Because there are so many more of them.

I fly –
like a bird,
And buzz –
like a bee,
Got a tail –
like a fish,
Got a hop –
like a flea.
A. Helicopter.

Q. How many lions can you put in an empty cage?
A. One – after that the cage will not be empty.

I walk all day through rain and snow;
I scuff through sleet and hail;
I sleep a-standing on my head;
And my name it rhymes with snail.
A. Nail in a shoe.

Mr Huddle,
Sitting in a puddle.
Green garters and yellow toes.
Tell me this riddle,
Or I'll smash your nose!
A. A duck.

Q. Why does a hen lay eggs?
A. Because if she let them drop, they would break.

Q. Why does a baby pig eat so much?
A. To make a hog of itself.

What organization!
He takes a trip
In a Morning Cloud,
Or a Statesmanship.

With canyon smile,
And cliff-side teeth,
This Honourable Gent,
Is . . .

A. Edward Heath.

Q. What's the best way to catch a fish?
A. Get someone to throw it to you.

Q. How can you avoid catching a cold?
A. Get the 'ell out of it.

Q. What's the best way to go fast asleep?
A. Do 100 mph with your eyes shut.

Q. Why did the King of France wear yellow suspenders on the First of May?
A. To keep his trousers up.

Q. Why did the boy throw the clock out of the window?
A. Because time was just standing still, and he wanted it to get a move on.

Old Father Boris, he came to my door,
He came with a dash, and a rush and a roar,
He whooped and he howled and he made a great din,
And at last the old fellow popped in.
A. North wind.

Q. How do we know God is male?
A. Because we sing hymns and not hers.

Q. What did the stag say to his children?
A. Hurry up, deer.

Q. What colour horse was King William riding at the battle of Hastings?
A. A chestnut – because that's when he conquered Harold.

Q. What did the Greek say when someone tore his trousers?
A. Euripides? Eumenides.

Q. When is a wall like a fish?
A. When it is scaled.

Q. What's a fur coat with a zip called?
A. A wind-cheetah.

Q. Christ never had one, but Napoleon did. Harold Wilson has one, but Edward Heath hasn't. What is it?
A. A wife.

Q. What country makes you shiver?
A. Chile.

Q. What river runs between two seas?
A. The Thames – between Chelsea and Battersea.

Q. What did Samson suffer from?
A. Fallen arches.

Q. Why didn't they use notebooks and pencils in Bible times?
A. Because the Lord told them to multiply on the face of the earth.

Q. Why couldn't Noah catch many fish while he was in the ark?
A. He only had two worms.

Q. When can you carry water in a sieve?
A. When it's frozen.

Q. Why was the farmer cross?
A. Because someone trod on his corn.

Q. Why is an archaeologist always unsuccessful?
A. Because his career lies in ruins.

Q. What is the hardest thing about learning to ride a bicycle?
A. The road.

Q. What is better than presence of mind in a car accident?
A. Absence of body.

Q. Why do some people press the lift button with their thumb, and others with their finger?
A. To signal for the lift.

Q. Do you believe in clubs for children?
A. Only when kindness fails.

Q. What is everyone in the world doing at the same time?
A. Growing older.

Q. If a girl falls down a well, why can't her brother help her out?
A. Because he can't be a brother and assist her too.

RIDDLES FROM AROUND THE WORLD

Most of these riddles are found all over the world, especially the first one which turns up with slight alterations again and again. Here are some that are known in many countries and then a few with the countries they came from. I expect you'll recognise quite a number of them.

> Four stiff-standers,
> Four dilly-danders,
> Two lookers,
> Two crookers,
> And a wig-wag.
> A. A cow.

> The children of Hong Kong,
>   Get money for making,
> What the children of England
>   Spend money for breaking.
> A. Toys.

Q. What is put on a table, cut, but never eaten?
A. A pack of cards.

Q. What has fingers but cannot use them?
A. Glove.

Formed long ago, yet made today,
   Employed while others sleep;
What few would like to give away,
   Nor any wish to keep.
A. Bed.

Its belly is a boat,
Its foot a paddle,
Its throat a trumpet.
A. Goose.

What is long and slim, works in the light,
Has but one eye, and an awful bite?
A. A needle.

Q. What is it that every man overlooks?
A. His nose.

Little Nancy Etticoat,
With a white petticoat,
And a red nose.
The longer she stands,
The shorter she grows.
A. Candle.

Q. See them going westward,
   All in a file,
   Trumpets, trumpets,
   And they blowing them.
A. Wild geese.

From Ireland

Q. A small low man down in the field,
    Wearing a big broad ruff,
    And having only one leg.

A. ˙ɯooɹɥsnW

From Iceland

        A certain maiden
        Jumped on the nose of Sir Aden.
        She did not know where to go –
        she jumped on the nose of Sir Snow.
        She did not know where to look –
        she jumped on the nose of Mr Cook.
        Men tried to catch her coat –
        she jumped down the bishop's throat.
        And she's still there –
        I know't!
        A. A fly.

Q. What is it,
   That falls down a cliff and doesn't break?
   Falls in the water and doesn't sink?
   Goes in the fire and doesn't burn?
A. Sunbeam.

From Norway

Q. A house full of grey wool,
   And you cannot get a fistful.
A. Smoke.

From Turkey

Q. I threw it from a minaret, and it didn't break,
   I threw it into the sea and it broke.
A. Paper.

MORE TEASERS

Q. What goes further the slower it goes?
A. Money.

Q. What has eyes and can't see, ears and can't hear, and
   can jump as high as Nelson's column?
A. A dead cat.

Q. But a dead cat can't jump?
A. Neither can Nelson's column!

Q. What will stay hot longest in the refrigerator?
A. Pepper.

Q. What is better to give than to receive?
A. Advice, kicks, and pills.

99

Four jolly men sat down to play,
And played all night till break of day;
They played for cash and not for fun,
And each could beat the other one.
But when they saw the finished score,
Each man had made some ten pounds more!
Can you this strange thing now explain,
How no one lost, and all could gain?
A. They were members of a pop group.

Q. Which floats best, tin or steel?
A. Tin can, but stainless steel sinks.

Q. What letter is never found in the alphabet?
A. The one in the post.

Q. Spell dry grass in 3 letters.
A. HAY

Q. Spell a hungry horse in 4 letters.
A. M T G G

Q. Why is there nothing like hay for when you're feeling faint?
A. Well, cold water would be better, but it's nothing like hay.

Q. What beats a good wife?
A. A bad husband.

Q. Why does a man allow himself to be hen-pecked?
A. Because he's chicken-hearted.

SOME MORE ALPHABET RIDDLES

Q. When can a donkey be spelled in one letter?
A. When it's U!

Q. How do you pronounce VOLIX?
A. Volume Nine.

Q. What letter travels the greatest distance?
A. D – because it goes to the end of the world.

Q. What letters are most like a Roman Emperor?
A. The C's are.

Q. What ends with E, and begins with P, and has a thousand letters?
A. Post Office.

Q. When were there only two vowels?
A. In the days of No-A, before U and I were born.

> My first is in table but not in chair,
> My second in den but not in lair.
> My third is in Pam, but not in Peter,
> My fourth is in Claire, but not in Rita.
> My fifth is in house and also in school,
> My sixth is in weapon but not in tool.
> My seventh's in rain, but not in snow,
> My whole is a figure that we all know.
> A. Teacher.

My first is in mud but not in bog,
My second's in wood and also in log.
My third is in yours, but not in mine,
My fourth is in sun, and also in shine.
My fifth is in here, and also in there,
And when you're not around I run everywhere.
What am I?
A. A mouse.

Q. Luke had it first, Paul had it last; boys never have it;
girls have it only once; Miss Sullivan had it twice in
the same place, but when she married Pat Murphy she
never had it again. What is it?
A. The letter L.

Q. What words can be pronounced quicker and shorter by
adding a syllable to them?
A. Quick and short.

Q. How could you say in one word that you had come across a doctor?
A. Metaphysician.

Q. Why is I the luckiest of vowels?
A. Because it is in the centre of happiness, while E is in hell, and all the others are in purgatory.

Q. What is the longest word in the English language?
A. SMILES – because it has a mile between the first and last letters.

Q. It is in the centre of gravity, and always invaluable;
   Out of tune, but the first to be vocal;
   Invisible, though clearly seen in the middle of a river;
   Three join it in vice; and three are in love with it;
   In vain you will look for it, for it has been in heaven a long time,
   And now lies in the grave?
A. The letter V.

Q. What is the longest sentence in the world?
A. Prison for life.

Q. Why is O the only vowel that is sounded?
A. Because all the others are inaudible (in AUDIBLE).

Q. My first is in head, but not in arm;
   My second is in field, but not in farm;
   My third is in true and also in brave;
   My fourth is in rescue, but not in save;
   My whole is a creature sprightly and gay
   And lives on the mountains, far away!
A. A deer.

Q. My first is in dove, but not in rook,
My second's in paper, but not in book.
My third is in lady, also in girl,
My fourth is in wavy, but never in curl.
My fifth is in narrow, but not in wide,
My sixth is in skate, but not in slide.
My seventh's in minute, but not in hour,
My eighth is in plant, but not in flower.
My ninth is in dinner, and also in tea –
Solve this – and send one to me!

A. A Valentine.

Q. Why are the 14th and 15th letters of the alphabet the most important of all?

A. Because we can't get ON without them.

Q. By equal division, strange to relate,
A half of thirteen you'll find to be eight.

A. Divide XIII in half by a horizontal line, and you get VIII.

Q. What's in the church, but not the steeple?
The parson has it, but not the people.

A. The letter R.

HEY DIDDLE RIDDLE

Q. If a monkey and a cockerel lost their knees, what would they do?

A. The monkey would go to the bank, and see if they still had any 'apennies, and the cockerel would go to London, because that's where cockneys are.

Q. A man was walking over a bridge when his hat blew off. What was his telephone number?

A. Avenue 1.

Q. And another man was walking over a bridge, and *his* hat blew off. What was his telephone number?

A. Avenue 12.

Q. If it took five men one day to dig up a field of cabbages, how long would it take seven men to dig the same field?

A. No time. It was done already.

Q. Four trains went out of a station; one went east, one went west, one went north and one went south. How many came back?

A. Three. One went west.

Q. A shepherd and his dog and a hundred sheep were in a field. How many feet did they have between them?

A. Two. (The dog has paws, and the sheep have trotters.)

Q. How many letters are there in the alphabet on December 25th?

A. Twenty-five, because that's when the angels said 'Noel'.

Q. If there are six birds on a tree, and a boy shoots one, how many are there left?

A. None. (The shot made the others fly away.)

Q. What relation is a doormat to a doorstep?

A. A step-farther.

Q. What happened when the sick man opened the window?

A. Influenza.

Knock, knock. Who's there?
Dr.
Dr Who?
That's right.

Knock, knock. Who's there?
Mr.
Mr Who?
Mr Bus-home.

Knock, knock. Who's there?
N.E.
N.E. who?
N.E.body you like, so long as you let me in.

Knock, knock. Who's there?
Ida.
Ida who?
Ida-terrible-time-getting-here.

Knock, knock. Who's there?
I.B.
I.B. who?
I.B. long-here.

Knock, knock. Who's there?
X.
X. who?
X-tremely glad to meet you.

Knock, knock. Who's there?
Ivor.
Ivor who?
Ivor-terrible-cold.
Well, Ivan-infectious-disease. Slam.

Knock, knock.
Knock, knock.
Ting-a-ling.
Who's there?
U.C.I.
U.C.I. who?
U.C.I.-had-to-ring, because you wouldn't answer when I knocked.

Knock, knock. Who's there?
Arthur.
Arthur who?
Arthur-any-more-biscuits?

Knock, knock. Who's there?
Sir.
Sir who?
Sir View-Wright.

Knock. knock. Who's there?
Isabel.
Isabel who?
Isabel necessary on a bicycle?

Knock, knock. Who's there?
Ewan.
Ewan who?
No, just me.

Knock, knock. Who's there?
Anna.
Anna who?
Anna Tomical.

Knock, knock. Who's there?
Flo.
Flo who?
Floating down the river.

Knock, knock, Who's there?
Fred.
Fred who?
Fred I'm late.

Q. What is it that never asks questions, but often has to be answered?
A. The door-bell.

Q. What prize did the man who invented door-knockers win?
A. The Nobel prize.

Q. Can a boy jump higher than a lamp-post?
A. Yes. Lamp-posts don't jump.

Q. Why is a Scots boy with a cold like a soldier on 7 days' leave?
A. Because they both have a wee cough (week off).

Q. What do you do if a herd of elephants charges at you?
A. Dial trunks and reverse the charge.

Q. What is striped and goes round and round?
A. A humbug in a revolving door.

Q. How did the baker get a shock?
A. He stood on a bun and a currant went up his leg.

Q. How do you stop a mole digging up your garden?
A. Hide the spade.

Q. Do you know the story about the butter?
A. No. Well, I won't tell you, because you might spread it.

Q. Why does a dog waggle its tail?
A. Because the tail cannot wag the dog.

Q. What should you do if you split your sides laughing?
A. Run until you get a stitch in them.

Q. Why was the woollen waistcoat marked 'Made of cotton'?
A. To fool the moths.

Q. How do you know a sausage doesn't like being fried?
A. Because it spits.

CRAZY RIDDLES

The man in the wilderness said to me,
How many strawberries grow in the sea?
I answered him as I thought good,
As many red herrings as grow in the wood.

What is yellow and very very dangerous?
Shark-infested custard.

What is orange and comes out of the ground at 100 mph?
An E-type carrot.

What happens when you drop a piano down a mineshaft?
A flat miner (minor).

How do you communicate with a fish?
Just drop him a line.

What's this man doing, leaning over the river-bank, holding
a fishing-line?
Teaching a worm to swim.

What is flat and yellow and goes round at $33\frac{1}{3}$ rpm?
A long-playing omelet.

What runs round Paris at lunch-time in a plastic bag?
The lunchpack of Notre Dame.

What leaves yellow footprints at the bottom of the sea?
A lemon sole.

What's made of wood, and swings from branch to branch?
A rocking-horse-fly.

And what's yellow, tastes of almonds, and swings from cake
to cake?
Tarzipan.

What's yellow, with greasy wings?
A bread and butterfly.

How do you hire a horse?
Put four bricks under it.

Who stands around all day eating sandwiches?
A loafer.

Why are the wolves howling?
Because they lost 3 nil to Manchester United.

What lies trembling at the bottom of the sea?
A nervous wreck.

What is white and fluffy and beats his chest in a cake shop?
A meringue-outingue.

WHAT CAN IT BE?

Q. What is it that was given to you, belongs only to you,
and yet your friends use it more than you do?
A. Your name.

Q. What is black and white and red all over?
A. An embarrassed zebra.

Q. What sticks closer than a brother?
A. A postage stamp, by gum!

Q. What is always running after another, but never catches
him?
A. The back wheel of a car.

Q. What is the strongest animal?
A. The snail, because it carries its house – an elephant only
carries a trunk.

> Goes over the fields all day,
> Sits in the larder all night.
> A. ꞰꞁᴉW

Q. What was the largest island before Australia was
discovered?
A. Australia.

Q. What can you cut with a knife, and never see where you cut it?
A. Water.

> What must have,
> The legs of a stag,
> The strength of a horse,
> The patience of a camel,
> The courage of an elephant,
> The stomach of a louse?
> A. A soldier.

Q. What's the best eavesdropper?
A. An icicle.

Q. How can you describe your lost parrot in one word?
A. Polygon.

Q. What would Neptune say if the sea dried up?
A. I haven't a notion (an ocean).

Q. What did the mouse say when it broke its tooth?
A. Hard cheese.

Q. What did the ground say when it began to rain?
A. If this goes on for long my name will be mud.

> I have one face,
> No ears or eyes,
> Two hands that round
> My face do rise.
> I sometimes strike
> Though never paid.
> I always stay where I am laid.
> A. Clock.

Q. Why did the owl 'owl?
A. Because the woodpecker would peck 'er.

Q. Why did the fly fly?
A. Because the spider spied 'er.

> White and thin;
> Red within;
> With a nail at the end.
> A. Finger.

Q. What do giraffes have that no other animals have?
A. Little giraffes.

Q. What are two rows of cabbages?
A. A dual cabbage-way.

Q. Why did the viper vipe 'er nose?
A. Because the adder 'ad 'er handkerchief.

Q. What did the ear 'ear?
A. Only the nose knows.

Q. How many sexes are there?
A. 3. Female sex, male sex, and insects.

Q. Why shouldn't you say buzz off, to a bee?
A. Because it's rude. Just say, 'Please begone'.

Q. What did the chestnut say when it knocked out another one?
A. I came, I saw, I conkered.

Q. Have you ever seen anyone opening a tin by just staring at it?
A. Yes. It was a real eye-opener.

Q. What's hot and tasty and found in the jungle?
A. Snake and pygmy pie.

Q. What did the ancient Egyptian boy say when his father was buried?
A. Goodbye mummy.

Q. What did the one-eared man answer, when he was offered a drink?
A. No thanks. I've got one 'ere.

Q. Why do you have to shout at a man with jelly in one ear and cream in the other?
A. Well, he'd be a trifle deaf, wouldn't he?

Q. What beats driving a Lotus at 150 mph?
A. Your heart, usually.

Q. What restaurant charges £5 a head?
A. A cannibal café.

Q. What's black and yellow and says zub, zub, zub?
A. A bee flying backwards.

Q. What's green and hairy and goes up and down?
A. A gooseberry in a lift.

Q. What's the difference between a buffalo and a bison?
A. Well, just try washing your hands in a buffalo.

Q. Why are a cock's feathers so smooth?
A. Because he carries a fine comb.

Q. Where can you find fish?
A. You can find a perch in a birdcage, a skate in a sports shop, and a sole on a shoe.

Q. Where did Noah strike the first nail in the ark?
A. On the head.

Q. What makes a pair of shoes?
A. Two shoes.

Q. What's the best way to get fat?
A. Go to the butcher.

Q. What has fifty heads but can't think?
A. A box of matches.

Q. When do elephants have eight feet?
A. When there are two of them.

Q. What is the last thing you take off when you go to bed?
A. Your feet off the floor.

Q. Who always goes to bed with his shoes on?
A. A horse.

Q. How can you close an envelope under water?
A. With a seal.

Q. Will your watch stop if it hits the floor?
A. Well, it wouldn't keep going, would it?

Q. What happens when you drive like lightning?
A. You strike trees.

Q. Why wasn't Eve afraid of catching measles?
A. Because she'd Adam.

Q. Why couldn't the church-tower keep a secret?
A. The bell always tolled.

Q. Why is the elephant that carried the Queen of Siam nothing whatever to do with the subject?
A. Because it's *her* elephant – and not her subject's.

Q. Why do we never have a moment to call our own?
A. Because the minutes are not hours.

RIDDLE SONGS

Lots of old ballads are full of riddles – here are just a few lines, (plus answers!) from one of them.

> Which is the maid without a tress?
> And which is the tower without a crest?
> (child in cradle: tower of Babel).

> Which is the water without any sand?
> And which is the king without any land?
> (water in the eyes: king in cards).

Where is no dust in all the road?
Where is no leaf in all the wood?
   (the milky way; fir-wood).

Which is the fire that never burnt?
And which is the sword without a point?
   (a painted fire: a broken sword).

Which is the house without a mouse?
Which is the beggar without a louse?
   (a snail's house: a painted beggar).

UPROARIOUS RIB-TICKLERS

Q. When is a black dog not a black dog?
A. When it's a greyhound.

Q. What has been since the world began, and yet is only
   one month old?
A. The moon.

Q. Why are wet pavements like music?
A. Because if you don't C-sharp, you will B-flat.

Q. Why is it hard to start a cricket game in the afternoon?
A. Because the bats like to sleep in the daytime.

Q. Why is a theatre such a sad place?
A. Because the seats are in tiers.

Q. What men are very strong?
A. Photographers; they are always developing.

Q. What are the largest kind of ants?
A. Gi-ants.

Q. Why is it hard to pull out a rotten tooth?
A. Because of the gravity of the cavity.

Q. What sort of noise does an earthquake make?
A. A howl in the ground.

Q. When does a cook not prepare a square meal?
A. When she wants it to go round.

Q. Why is my cup of tea stronger than yours?
A. Because it's all my tea (almighty).

Q. If cheese comes after dinner, what comes after cheese?
A. A mouse.

Q. What does a poultry farmer drink?
A. Cocktails.

Q. Why is a fishmonger such a mean man?
A. Because his business makes him sell-fish.

Q. When you look round on a cold winter's day, what do you see on every hand?
A. A glove.

Q. How do you start a bear race?
A. Ready, Teddy, Go!

Q. What bill never needs paying?
A. A duck's bill.

Q. What is it that is too much for one, enough for two, and nothing at all for three?
A. A secret.

Q. How do you start a flea race?
A. One – two – flea – Go!

Q. How much luggage did the animals take into the Ark?
A. Well, the fox and cock only had a brush and comb between them.

Q. How did the frog die?
A. He croaked it.

Q. When is a winter storm like a child with a cold?
A. When it blows, it snows (its nose).

Q. Who has no control over her pupils?
A. A cross-eyed teacher.

Q. What is the best way to make a fire with two sticks?
A. Make sure one of them is a match.

Q. When is a pie like a poet?
A. When it is Browning.

Q. If a woman were to change sex, why couldn't she be a Christian?
A. Because she'd be a he then.

Q. Why do cows wear cowbells?
A. Because their horns don't work.

Q. Can you tell me of what parentage Napoleon Bonaparte was?
A. Of Corsican.

Q. If it takes 3 men 9 hours to dig a hole 9 feet square, how long would it take one man to dig half a hole?
A. There ain't no such thing.

Q. When is a man like frozen rain?
A. When he's hale.

Q. Why is a boy who talks too much like a young pig?
A. Because he'll turn into a great bore (boar).

Q. Why must birds in a nest always agree?
A. To keep from falling out.

Q. Why is an underfed dog like a philosopher?
A. Because he's a thin cur (thinker).

Q. What's a lawyer's favourite pudding?
A. Sue-it.

Q. What's the least dangerous kind of robbery?
A. Safe robbery.

Q. What paper is full of news about you?
A. Tissue paper.

Q. What is red and white, has 22 legs and 2 wings?
A. Manchester United.

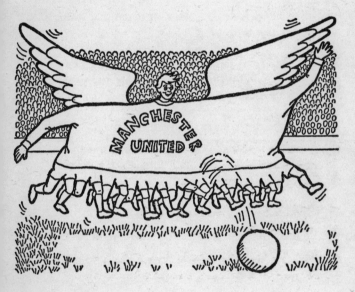

Q. What did one sheep say to the other, by the gate?
A. After ewe.

Q. What is black, round, and does 40 knots?
A. An oilskin button with an outboard motor.

Q. What can you wear over two years, and you can wear it out too, but it can still look as good as new?
A. A hat.

Q. Why is a bad boy like a field of wheat?
A. They both get thrashed.

Q. What do people always cry over?
A. Onions.

Q. Why do you never starve at the seaside?
A. Because of the sand which is there.

Q. What happened when the rash man ate a rasher?
A. He became a cannibal.

Q. If a man is on top of a monument with a live goose in his arms, what is the quickest way for him to get down?
A. Pluck the goose.

Q. What did the monkey say when someone cut off his tail?
A. It won't belong now.

Q. What runs all the way from San Francisco to New York without moving?
A. A railway line.

Q. Four monks kept a fish and chip shop. What was their number?
A. Blackfriars 1234.

Q. What must you keep after giving it to someone else?
A. Your word.

BACK SLANG
Answers to pages 60–61

Once upon a time there was a little girl. What was her name?
Sicily.

This little girl was frightfully thin. What country did she live in?
Finland.

Her mother saw her crying. What did the mother say?
'Are you Hungary?'

What did the child answer?
'Yes, Siam.'

What did Sicily ask her mother then?
'Kenya give me something to eat?'

What did the mother give her to eat?
A slice of Turkey.

But Sicily started to cry again. Why was that?
She wanted Samoa.

What did the mother say this time?
'Oh, for goodness sake, stop those Wales.'

And when Sicily still went on making a nasty noise, what did her mother say?
'Denmark my words. Do as you are told, or I will give you a Tanzania.'

'What is THAT?'

Sicily did not wait to find out. What did she say?
'Iran away.'

The trick with Back Slang is to take the first letter of the word and transfer it to the end, adding 'ay'. If the word begins with a vowel, leave it alone, but add 'yay'. Words made up of two separate words, like 'understand', are treated as if they are two words, 'under' and 'stand'. If a word begins with a double consonant, like 'wh', move *both* of them to the end of the word.

If you have enjoyed this Piccolo book,
you may like to choose your next book from
the titles listed on the following pages

Piccolo puzzles and games

Margaret Gossett
Piccolo Book of Jokes (illus) 20p

Farmer: What do you use to treat a pig with a sore throat?
Vet: Oinkment.

The best way to treat yourself – to a good laugh! – is with
this hilarious collection of Jokes, Howlers, Limericks, Puns
and Shaggy Dog stories. But be warned! Piccolo Books
can't be held responsible for the consequences if you laugh
out loud while reading this book in public!

Alvin Schwartz
Tomfoolery (illus) 30p

Tricks with words to trip you up and muddle your friends.

Witcracks (illus) 30p

Jokes of all sorts: riddles, puns, ancient jokes, modern jokes,
and even 'Confucius say' jokes.

These two books by Alvin Schwartz are a load of laughs for
everyone!

Piccolo puzzles and games

Have you noticed the fiendish tricks of Gobfrey Shrdlu recently? He's always making mischief (so says Denys Parsons!) – causing all those unfortunate printing errors, grammatical slips and double meanings that give the printer a terrible headache but make us just double up! Like –

'Steel-wool toilet rolls 2½p each.'
(Hardware advert)

'The match was unfinished owing to measles. Craghurst was compelled to scratch.'
(The Harrovian)

'If the surface is tough, give it two goats.'
(Practical Householder)

'Break the eggs carefully into a basin, taking care not to break the eggs.'
(Cookery Book)

Denys Parsons's hilarious collections of Howlers and Misprints are guaranteed to keep you and your friends in fits of laughter!

Fun-Tastic (illus) 25p
Even More Fun-Tastic (illus) 20p

Piccolo Puzzles and games

Nut-Crackers (illus) 20p
John Jaworski and Ian Stewart

Meet Professor Crankshaft, the only professor who invents
impossible objects. Professor Crankshaft is full of surprises –
just like this book. It's the zippiest, zaniest, merry-go-round
of fun and games you've ever known.

In between the Professor's hilariously astonishing inventions
is a crackerjack collection of word games, string puzzles,
mazes, codes, number patterns, skeleton crosswords and
much, much more besides.